CHILDREN'S ESL CURR.____

LEARNING ENGLISH WITH LAUGHTER

PRACTICE BOOK 2A: CASTLES AND THINGS

Second Edition Black and White

An Interactive Ready to Use Approach to Teaching English to Children.

This Black and White Series Includes a Student Book, Practice Book, and a Teacher's Guide with a Final Test.

The Children Will Listen, Repeat, Participate in Reading Activities, Games, Rhymes and Printing.

George and Daisy Stocker
Learning English with Laughter Ltd.
Victoria, B.C. Canada
V8X 3B6
E-mail: info@successfulesl.com

CHILDREN'S ESL CURRICULUM

ISBN-13: 978-1494495220

ISBN-10: 1494495228

Published by:
Learning English with Laughter Ltd.
10 – 1030 Hulford Street
Victoria, B.C. Canada V8X 3B6
Visit us on the Web at:
ESL Curriculum: **http://www.successfulesl.ca**
Successful ESL: **http://www.esl-curriculum.ca**
English for Chinese: **http://www.englishforchinese.ca**
Printed in the USA

Customization of your covers

You may be interested in the customization of your covers. (White Label Services)
This personalizes your textbooks and makes them a visible part of your school's curriculum.
For this service contact us at: info@successfulesl.com

Members of our team with professional degrees have combined years of teaching experience and editing to produce these teaching materials.
Team Members for this publication:
Editors:
Daisy A. Stocker B.Ed., M.Ed.
Dr. George A. Stocker D.D.S.

CHILDREN'S ESL CURRICULUM

A "LEARNING ENGLISH WITH LAUGHTER" PUBLICATION

PRACTICE BOOK 2A: CASTLES AND THINGS

Second Edition: Black and White

Originally Copyrighted 2007
Second Edition Copyrighted 2013,
Learning English With Laughter Ltd.
10 – 1030 Hulford Street
Victoria, B.C. Canada V8X 3B6
website: http://www.esl-curriculum.ca

Learning English with Laughter Ltd.
Daisy A. Stocker B.Ed., M.Ed. and George Stocker D.D.S
1030 Hulford Street
Victoria, B.C., Canada, V8X 3B6
http://www.esl-curriculum.ca
e-mail: learning@efl-esl.com

CHILDREN'S ESL CURRICULUM

PRACTICE BOOK 2A: CASTLES AND THINGS

STUDENT'S BOOK

This is written for children under the age of eight. It is assumed that they will have been introduced to the alphabet, beginning consonant sounds, and short vowel sounds. This book reviews beginning sounds and sound symbol associations. It introduces rhyming words, numbers from 11 to 20, a new vocabulary of about 200 words, role-plays and many verses that the children will repeat many times. These activities provide practice with speaking and identifying rhyming words while introducing basic sentence structure and the rhythm of the English language.

The basic teacher instructions are given in the small boxes on each page. This is efficient for the teacher and also allows the parents to understand what the child has been asked to do. For this reason, the instructions are more repetitive and detailed than would be necessary if they were for teacher use only. It is important that the teacher repeat each question and guide the children's sentence answers many times. In this way the children are learning basic sentence structure and grammar.
We suggest that the students use paper markers of about 17 centimeters long and 5 centimeters wide to help them to attend to the relevant section of the page. These are attractive if they are made of colored paper or cardboard. Having a class set of laminated cards saves time and money.

PRACTICE BOOK

This book provides independent work for the children. The students will need a brief explanation of what they are to do before starting the pages that accompany each lesson.
Each student travels with the storybook characters and a classroom or an imaginary friend. The activities include drawing, printing and reading. The instructions are supplied in **bold face** to direct the children to what they are expected to do. Some pages have brief small print instructions for the teacher.

TEACHER'S GUIDE

This Guide provides a review of rhyming words and some of the vocabulary introduced in the previous books. Also, Book 1B has many simple verses that are provided in this Guide for the teacher to refer to. The games provided in this Guide provide essential listening and speaking activities that reinforce the lessons covered in the book. They are a very important part of the program.
If your students are starting Book 2A without completing Books 1A and 1B of this series, we suggest you look at Game 1 of this Guide.

TEACHING PHILOSOPHY

This series is introducing English as a second language to young children. They are learning to understand, speak, read and write. As young children view their world as a whole, rather than in parts, an integrated approach is used. The activities include grammar, phonics, listening, verses, speaking and printing. Graphics are used extensively to promote understanding, and are integrated with the speaking, reading and writing activities.

Note: You are the teacher – do it your way!
We wish you success with your classes,
Daisy Stocker B.Ed. M.Ed.   George Stocker D.D.S.
Learning English with Laughter Ltd.

CHILDREN'S ESL CURRICULUM
STUDENT BOOK 2A

CASTLES AND THINGS

CONTENTS:
These Pages Refer to Student Book 2A

CHILDREN'S ESL CURRICULUM

INDEX OF PHONICS

BOOK 2A: CASTLES AND THINGS
The Page Numbers Below Refer to Student Book 2A

LESSON 1:   BEHIND THE CASTLE WALL

Draw the castle with the flag of your country.

My friends and I
made a castle tall,

_____

_____

_____

_____

The children are to choose the answer from the box.	**Do you build castles?**

_____

_____

Yes, I build castles.   No, I don't build castles.

Draw the tall brave king.

The king is tall and
brave and bold.

Are you brave?

| Yes, I'm brave. | No, I'm not brave. |

THE KING PATROLS HIS WOODS
Draw the king on his horse.

Do you see any thieves?

You: _____

The children choose their answer from the box below.

Yes, I do.

No, I don't.

The king patrols beside the woods.

_____

_____

_____

Draw the thieves hiding in the woods.

How many thieves did you draw?

one   two   three   four   five   six   seven   eight

I drew _____ thieves.

The woods where the
thieves are able to hide.

_____

_____

_____

_____

THE QUEEN
Draw the cakes on the table.

The queen was merry
and often sat,

_____
_____
_____
_____

At a table of cakes
that made her fat.

_____
_____
_____
_____

www.esl-curriculum.ca

You are meeting the queen. **Draw yourself.**

I meet the queen.
She is friendly.

_____

_____

_____

_____

Is the queen friendly?

_____

_____

_____

| Yes, she's friendly. | No, she isn't friendly. |

THE QUEEN'S MAIDS

Draw the queen.   She calls her maids.

Maids!

Maids!

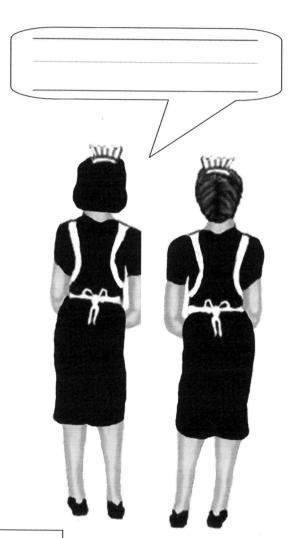

We're coming!

The merry fat queen
calls for her maids.

Draw your friend doing the queen's hair.

When dinner is finished
she calls for her maids.

_____
_____
_____
_____

THE PRINCE
Draw a dragon that spits fire.

The prince, he hunts
for dragons long,

He's not afraid
because he's strong.

The prince and I
hunt dragons.

Draw yourself on the horse.

We aren't afraid!!

A DRAGON

The prince saves the princess.

Oh, thank you!

Print the words:

prince

princess

king

queen

maid

THE PRINCESS
Where does the princess run?
Draw the princess.

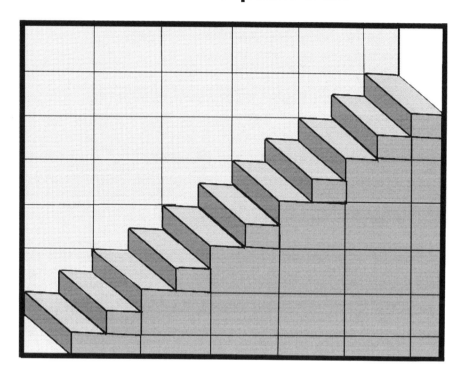

The princess runs
on the castle stairs.

With her beautiful dress
and her long black hair.

You meet the princess.

Hello! How are you?

Draw yourself.

Print what you say.

Hello, Princess	I'm fine, thank you.

The students are to choose and print words from the box that tells what they would answer.

AT THE TOP OF THE TOWER

Hello!

I want to climb the tower.

I want to visit the Princess.

Draw what you do.
What did you do?

_____

_____

_____

| I climbed to | I visited the |

The students are to choose the words in the box to begin their sentence and copy what they would say from the story character's words.

The children are to choose the beginning of their sentence from the words in the box and complete their sentence from the words that the storybook characters say.

Your friend can climb my towers.

Your friend can visit my gardens.

I'll ask my friend.

That would be cool!

1. What will your friend do?

_____

_____

_____

My friend will climb to
My friend will visit the

Draw what your friend will do.

_____

THE CIRCUS
Draw yourself and your friends playing with the band.

Did you like playing in the band?

Yes, I liked playing.
No, I didn't like playing.

When the circus

band is playing

It always

makes me sing.

1. Would you want to be a clown?

2. Would you want to be a conductor?

3. Would you want to play
   in the band?

4. Would you want to play the drum?

| Yes, I would. | No, I wouldn't. |

The children are to choose their answer from the box.

Print what the clown does.

_____

_____

Print what the girl does.

_____

_____

_____

_____

The girl rides the elephant.
The clown rides the horse.

Draw yourself having
a good ride on the horse.

The children are to print the
sentences from the box beside
the corresponding picture.

THE LIONS

The lions crouch,
then do their tricks.

_____

. . . .

_____

. . . .

_____

Jumping through hoops
and over sticks.

_____

. . . .

_____

. . . .

_____

Draw yourself jumping through a hoop.

Can you crouch like
a lion?

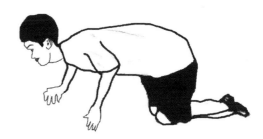

_____

_____

_____

**Draw yourself
crouching.**

You are crouching like a lion.

Can your friend jump
through a hoop?

**Draw your friend jumping
through a hoop.**

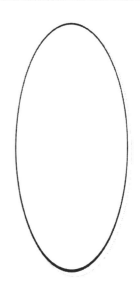

_____

_____

_____

Yes, my friend can.   No, my friend can't.

THE ELEPHANT

Draw what you think the clown will do.

Did the clown do a trick?

Yes, he did a trick.
No, he didn't do a trick.

_____

_____

_____

Sitting on an elephant

Would you sit on its neck?

Would you sit on its trunk?

Would you sit on its back?

Where would you sit on an elephant?

_____

_____

_____

| I would sit on its neck.
I would sit on its back.
I would sit on its trunk. |

Draw yourself on this elephant:

THE ACROBATS

The acrobats
swing all about.

Draw yourself on a swing.

They always
make the
people shout.

Print the words:

clown

pony

lion

elephant

acrobat

THE CLOWNS

The clowns are
running to and fro.

_____
_____
_____
_____

Draw what the clowns will do.

They ran.
They jumped.
They ran and
jumped.

What did they do?

_____
_____
_____

The clown runs
from the lion!

_____

_____

_____

_____

Draw yourself running from a lion.

_____

_____

_____

Help me!

I run fast!

I'm strong!

THE CIRCUS CAR

Draw your friends in the car.

The children print their friend's names after the sentence provided.

Who did you draw in the car?

I drew

The prince rides on a horse.

The king rides in a

_____

_____

_____

car

The lady clown rides on a

_____

_____

_____

giraffe

The chimp rides on a

_____

_____

_____

lion

I ride on a

_____

_____

_____

pony

The children choose
words to complete
the sentences.

Made in the USA
San Bernardino, CA
24 August 2018